MASTERING ADOBE ILLUSTRATOR 2024

BEGINNERS GUIDE FOR MASTERING DIGITAL DESIGN WITH ADOBE ILLUSTRATOR

SOPHIA RYAN

TABLE OF CONTENT

CHAPTER 1

UNDERSTANDING ADOBE ILLUSTRATOR

For anyone wishing to create drawings, illustrations, and artwork on a Windows or MacOS computer, Adobe Illustrator is a necessary tool. Many designers, illustrators, and artists use this software to create visually spectacular works of art. Illustrator is unique because it can create vector graphics, which are a versatile kind of digital art. This changes everything from intricate logos to striking billboards since it allows you to scale your graphics up or down without sacrificing quality.

For everyone wishing to create drawings, illustrations, and artwork on a Windows or MacOS computer, Adobe Illustrator is a necessary application. Many designers, painters, and illustrators use this program to create amazing images. Illustrator is unique in that it can create vector graphics, which are a versatile kind of digital art. This is revolutionary for everything from intricate logos to striking billboards since it allows you to scale your graphics up or down without sacrificing quality.

The enormous selection of drawing tools available to you in Adobe Illustrator is one of its most fascinating features. To bring your ideas to life, you'll find brushes, shapes, and patterns to help you sketch quickly or create detailed designs. Working with text is another fantastic use for Illustrator; you may change the letter alignment, spacing, and style to suit your artistic requirements.

Another important benefit is the program's smooth interface with other Adobe Creative Cloud programs, such as Photoshop and InDesign. Because of this connectedness, integrating Illustrator projects into larger design projects is simple and streamlines your process.

To sum up, Adobe Illustrator is a flexible and strong tool that enables you to express your ideas and create designs of high caliber. Illustrator is a priceless tool for realizing your ideas, regardless of your level of experience.

UNDERSTANDING THE INTERFACE

You may achieve your creative goals with a variety of tools and capabilities available in the Adobe Illustrator interface, which is a powerful and flexible work environment. Let us go over the main components of the interface to help you better grasp how to utilize and navigate it.

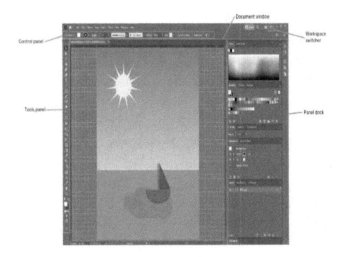

PLEASE NOTE: The Illustrator interface you see above may not look precisely like the diagram above, depending on the workspace you're using.

The outlined points in the accompanying image will be discussed.

SETTING UP DOCUMENT PREFERENCES

Prior to using Adobe Illustrator, setting document preferences is a crucial step. Panel and command positions are saved in an Illustrator preferences file that opens with Illustrator. A host of other application settings are also kept in the preference file, such as options for general display, file-saving, performance, type, plug-ins, and scratch disks. The Preferences dialog box allows you to adjust the majority of these settings. When you close an application, your preference settings are kept.

Abnormal conduct could suggest distorted inclinations. Replace preferences with their original settings if you think there may have been harm to them.

1. First, go to the Preferences.
2. Open an existing document or start a new one in Adobe Illustrator.
3. Select Editor > Preferences (Mac) or Edit > Preferences (Windows).

As an alternative, you can open the Preferences panel by observing the following steps:

1. keyboard shortcuts Ctrl + K (Windows) or Command + K (Mac).
2. Configuring Broad Preferences Choose the General category from the Preferences menu.
3. Adjust the Units to the measuring unit of your choice such as points, inches, centimeters, etc.
4. Select the color mode that you want (e.g., RGB, CMYK, Grayscale, etc.).

5. Decide the artboard options (preset sizes, bespoke sizes, etc.) you desire.
6. Choosing Your Artboard Preferences Choose the category for Artboard Options.
7. Enter the number of artboards you wish to have. decide on the size and orientation of your desired artboard (landscape, portrait, etc.).
8. Enter the required values for the Artboard Spacing and Columns. Configuring Snap and Grid Preferences Choose the Grid group.
9. Enter the desired values for the Grid Size and Subdivisions. Select the Snap to Grid options (snapshot to pixel, snap to grid, etc.) that you desire. Choose the desired value for the Snap Tolerance. Establishing Rules and Regulators' Choices Choose the category for Guides & Rulers.
10. Select the measuring unit of your choice using the Ruler Units. Select the guide options (such as show guides, lock guides, etc.) that you desire. Choose the color you want for the Guide Color.

Choosing a Type Preference:

1. Choose the category for Type, Choose the font preview size that you want. Select the Font Substitution alternatives that you like.
2. Select the text engine that you want to use.

Configure Preferences for Exporting and Saving. To configure preference, do the following:

a) Decide on the category for file handling.
b) Modify the Save As parameters (file format, version, etc.).

c) Select the export settings that you want (e.g., file format, resolution, etc.).

Configuring further Preferences:

a) Examine further categories (such as Plug-ins, User Interface, etc.) and adjust the settings to suit your requirements.

Keep Your Preferences Safe;

1. Press OK to store your selections.
2. All upcoming documents will take your preferences into account.

Your productivity will be streamlined and your creative experience will be improved by customizing your document options in Adobe Illustrator by using these methods. Panel and command positions are saved in an Illustrator preferences file that opens with Illustrator. A host of other application settings are also kept in the preference file, such as options for general display, file-saving, performance, type, plug-ins, and scratch disks. The Preferences dialog box allows you to adjust the majority of these settings. When you close an application, your preference settings are kept. Abnormal conduct could suggest distorted inclinations. Replace preferences with their original settings if you think there may have been harm to them.

EXPLORING TOOLS AND PANELS USING THE TOOLS PANEL

In addition to color adjustments and a screen mode menu, the Tools panel has 77 tools for creating and manipulating objects. To reveal the Tools panel if it's hidden, select Window > Tools. You can drag the top (dark gray) bar to reposition the Tools panel.

To pick a similar tool from a pop-out menu, click and hold on a tool with a small arrowhead. Alternatively, click once to select an available tool. Double-clicking a tool will open the associated settings dialog box. Examples of these tools are the Paintbrush and Pencil tools.

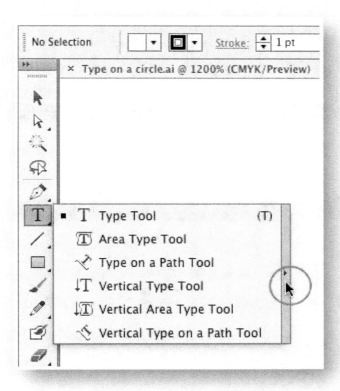

To make a tearoff toolbar that stands alone, A–B To access the tool pop-out menu on the far right side, click the arrowhead and release the mouse when it crosses the vertical tearoff bar. Drag the upper bar of a tearoff toolbar to move it. A tearoff toolbar's close box can be clicked to bring it back to the Tools panel.

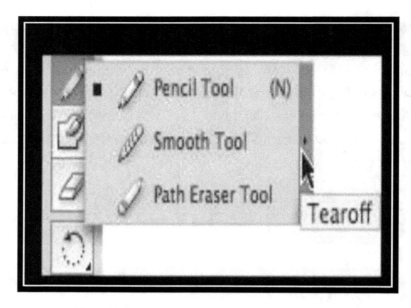

Open a tearoff toolbar by choosing a tearoff bar.

A tearoff bar is created below

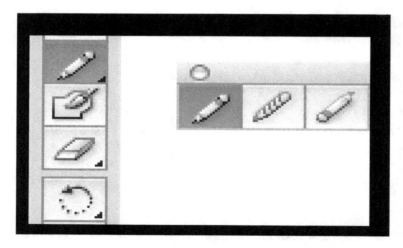

Study the diagram below showing the various segment of tools panel critically.

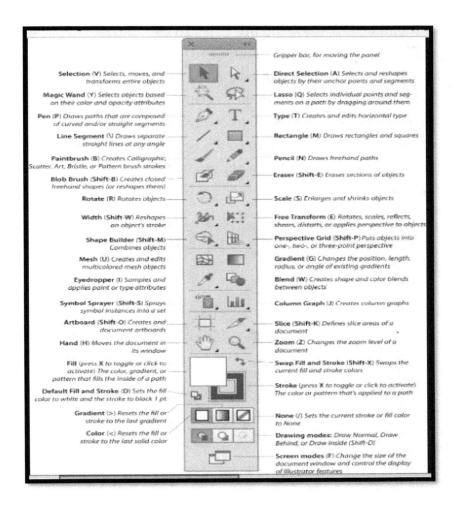

A tearoff bar is created

NAVIGATING ARTBOARDS

An artboard in Illustrator is essentially a piece of white paper that serves as the foundation for your creative work. To develop your artwork, you can make custom-sized artboards or use the presets that are offered for common devices. Additionally, you can print or export them. You can add or make more than one artboard if you have multiple designs. Artboards can also be removed, duplicated, renamed, and resized to suit your needs.

Which three Illustrator artboard navigation methods are there? You can double-click an artboard's name in the Artboards panel. You can use the Artboard Navigation arrows in the lower-left of the Document window to navigate to the first, previous, next, and last artboard. You can select the artboard number from the Artboard Navigation menu at the bottom-left of the Document window.

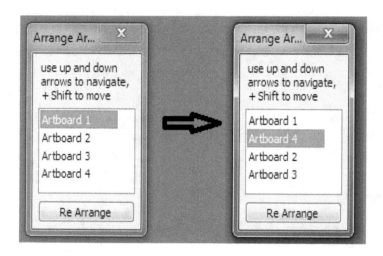

1. we fire up the script
2. move artboard 4, underneath artboard 1
3. press Re Arrange button

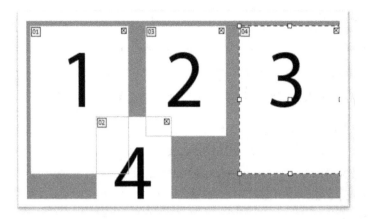

The new order is now 1,4,2,3 for navigating

NB: While an artboard's default name reflects its starting number, this is only a label. To change the name of an artboard, click its label or use the artboards panel settings menu. This can be done while the artboard tool is active.

By moving a row up or down to the desired place, you can rearrange the artboards listed in the Artboards panel (Ctrl + SHIFT + O). This makes the artboards a new number. Fantastic for exporting—you can stop constantly rearranging PDF pages.

INTRODUCTION TO VECTOR GRAPHICS

Computer visuals known as vector graphics are produced by arranging lines and objects in two or three dimensions through a series of commands or mathematical formulas.

The most common types of vector file are:

- AI (Adobe Illustrator),
- EPS (Encapsulated PostScript),
- PDF (Portable Document Format)

- SVG (Scalable Vector Graphics).

Using vector images instead of raster ones has advantages and disadvantages. benefits of photos in vector format. Among the main advantages of vector files are:

1. A limitless resolution: You can produce a vector image almost any size you want without sacrificing resolution. In contrast, raster files are only preserved in resolution when they are resized to a predetermined size. The more you stretch them, the more likely it is the quality will suffer.
2. Reduced file sizes: Compared to raster photographs, which might include a lot of camera data, vector files are often lighter since they don't contain blocks of pixels.
3. Ample features in the design. Vector graphics have several drawbacks. You cannot edit them. You cannot add shapes, text, colors or filters.

The following are some drawbacks of utilizing vector files:
- Less helpful for intricate pictures.
- Since each pixel in a raster format can be altered, highly detailed digital photographs might work better in this format. Generally speaking, vector files work better for graphics than for photos. the compatibility problems.
- To open and work on vector files, you'll need a vector-based design program such as Adobe Illustrator. Using raster-based tools to edit vectors can be challenging.
- Issues with conversion.
- Because it takes more processing power, converting a raster image to a vector file is typically far more difficult than the other way around.

- Produce original artwork and designs that you can readily change time and again.

vector graphics images below

PowerPoint presentation on vector graphic art

Process vector icon

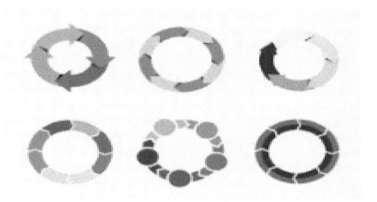

WORKING WITH LAYERS

Layers are like transparent folders holding artwork. You can alter the arrangement of the objects in your artwork by rearranging the folders. Subfolders can be created within folders, and things can be moved between folders.

Using layers, you may divide up your work into separate sections that can be altered and seen as separate pieces. There are layers in every Adobe Illustrator document. You can simply manage how your artwork is printed, displayed, and modified by adding numerous layers to it. Each new document has a single layer by default, and all of the objects you create are listed beneath that layer. To better fit your needs, you can rearrange the objects and add new layers.

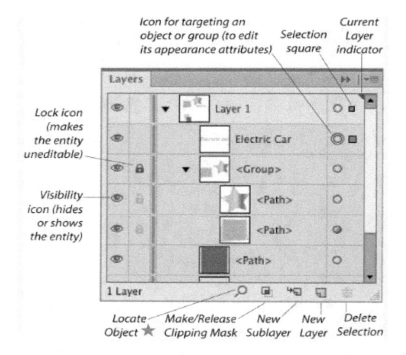

Illustrating how layers are displayed

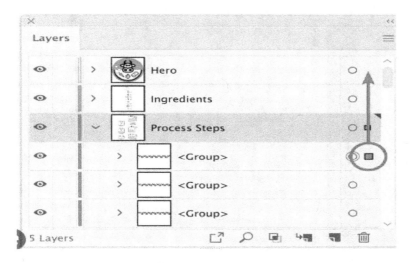

Layer order diagram

CUSTOMIZING WORKSPACE AND KEYBOARD SHORTCUTS

Take the following actions to personalize your workspace:

1. Click the Edit menu and choose Keyboard Shortcuts from the list that drops down.

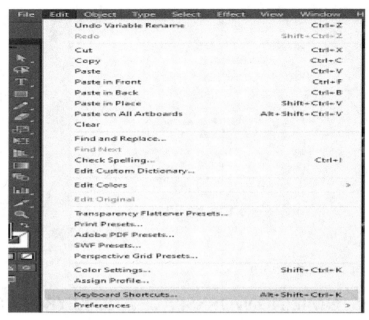

2. After the dialogue box for keyboard shortcuts opens, you can select a set of shortcuts from the set menu.

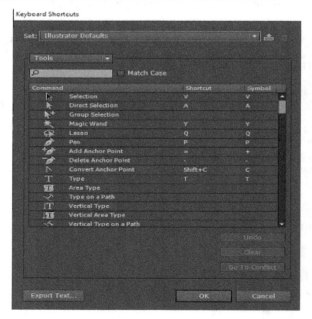

3. Select a shortcut type from the menu that appears above the shortcut display.

Default Keyboard Shortcuts

Working	Windows	Mac OS
Undo	Ctrl + Z	Command + Z
Redo	Shift + Ctrl + Z	Shift + Command + Z
Cut	Ctrl + X	Command + X
Copy	Ctrl + C	Command + C
Paste	Ctrl + V	Command + V
Paste in front	Ctrl + F	Command + F
Paste at back	Ctrl + B	Command + B
Paste in place	Shift + Ctrl + B	Shift + Command + B
Paste on all artboards	Alt + Shift + Ctrl + B	Option + Shift + Command + B
Check spelling	Ctrl + I	Command + I
Open the Color Settings dialog box	Shift + Ctrl + K	Shift + Command + K
Open the Keyboard Shortcuts dialog box	Alt + Shift + Ctrl + K	Option + Shift + Command + K
Open the Preferences dialog box	Ctrl + K	Command + K

CHAPTER 2

BASIC DRAWING TECHNIQUES

By applying the proper drawing technique and tool, these drawing instruments are employed to make a drawing. The most popular drawing supplies include crayons, graphite pencils, ink pens, and charcoal.

Basic drawings are as follows;

The two primary types of basic shapes are solid and planar figures. Plane figures are two-dimensional objects that are positioned on a single plane with dimensions of length and width. Quadrilaterals, squares, rectangles, triangles, and circles are a few types of plane figures.

Here is an explanation of the foundation:

1. The foundation of each artwork is a point and line The simplest drawing tools are the point and the line. A motif's outline is shown by the line. Drawing boundaries and object outlines is done using this fundamental approach. It can be used to highlight and illustrate contrasts. Besides that, the point can be used as a drawing tool.

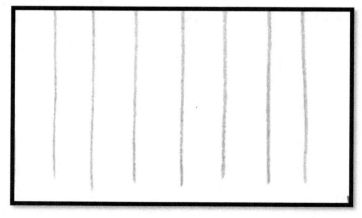

The lines basic drawing tool.

2. The hatching: The surfaces of a motif can be drawn and formed using this age-old drawing method. The sketching technique known as "hatching" produces thin lines. The major outline and the line direction are usually at an oblique angle. Simple hatching, cross hatching, and cross hatching in the dimension are the three types of hatching that we have.

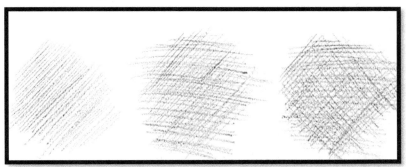

3. Smudging approach: You can use your finger or an instrument like as cotton wool, a cloth, a cotton swab, an eraser, a brush, or a paper wiper (or tortillion) to draw with this approach. You already work at the drawing's edge when you use the smudging approach. Another traditional method of combining drawing techniques is the use of watercolor paints or opaque white to create sparkly lights in the drawing.

4. Combination techniques: They alter materials, techniques, and procedures while straddling the lines between traditional painting and drawing techniques.

5. Combination drawing techniques: They fluctuate in materials, methods, and procedures, straddling the boundaries between traditional painting and drawing approaches.

DRAWING SHAPES

For many creative endeavors, drawing serves as the basis. To convey their ideas and goals, the majority of talented illustrators use a variety of drawing techniques. Illustrator's shape tools enable you to easily and precisely construct basic shapes. Additionally, you may alter shapes created with these tools dynamically without having to transition to a new tool because the majority of them are live shapes.

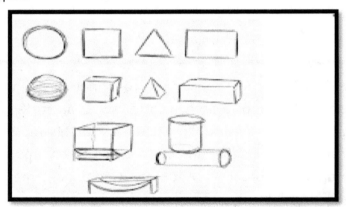

Which five forms are fundamental to drawing?
The geometric shapes—triangles, squares, rectangles, circles, and ellipses—are the five fundamental shapes in art. You may make other more complicated shapes, like polygons or combinations of circles and rectangles, using these five fundamental shapes.
Drawing types:
- Cartoon drawings. Oversimplified or overly dramatic depictions of subjects are known as caricature drawings.

- Cartoon drawings usually present a whimsy or humorous interpretation of reality. Like caricatures, they could employ exaggerated shapes and colors to convey tone or emotion through visuals.
- Drawing figures, sometimes referred to as still lifes, involves making observations of the real world. Though they can also be inanimate objects like fruit, cars, or natural objects, subjects are typically human models.
- Sketching gestures Real-world subjects serve as inspiration for gesture drawing. But gesture drawing is more concerned with movement, attempting to capture form, activity, and pose. To simulate mobility, models or participants frequently switch positions every one to five minutes.
- Sketching in lines Using only straight lines and contours without any shading is the main goal of line drawing. Most of the time, a line drawing artist creates the entire image without ever using an instrument.
- Drawing in perspective Anamorphic drawing, also known as 3D drawing, is a technique used to produce three-dimensional representations in a two-dimensional space, like on paper, by taking into account factors like surface, scale, light, volume, and distance between objects.
- Photorealism, sometimes known as hyperrealism, is the idea of creating a drawing that appears so realistic that it could be taken as a picture. Although it may be applied to drawings as well, pointillism is a painting technique that is more frequently used. It creates a realistic image with light and shadows when viewed from a distance by employing the stippling technique to create a large number of tiny dots.

WORKING WITH THE PEN TOOL

Anchor points are added to a canvas or picture in order for the Pen Tool to function. Segments that are curved or straight can be formed by joining these anchor locations. Users can alter the path's curvature and contour by manipulating the anchor points' control handles.

Tips for Using Photoshop's Pen Tool:

- Draw forms and lines. Set two anchor points to form straight line.
- Heart Attack and Stroke. Use the Stroke Path option when you right-click (on PCs) or control-click (on Macs) on your path to outline the path you constructed.
- Conceal a layer.
- Make decisions.

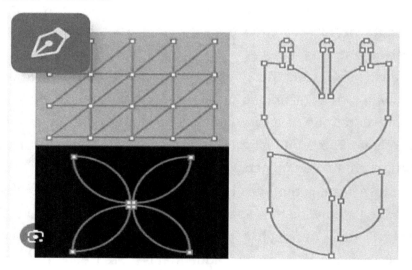

What is the type of pen tool and how is it used?

A route creator is the pen tool. You may make slick trails that you can use a brush to stroke or apply to a selection. This tool works well for layout, creating, and choosing smooth surfaces. When editing a document with Adobe Illustrator, the paths can also be utilized in that program.

PEN TOOL USES

1. Writing is done with a pen.

2. The pen can be a kids' "telescope" toy or used as a straw.

3. The bicycle lock is unlocked with a pen.

4. Simply remove the ink tube, place a tiny paper scroll inside, and replace the ink to send and keep hidden messages.

5. You can make a chandelier with the pen.

Keyboard shortcuts for the Pen Tool:

- Pen Tool use. Using the Direct Selection Tool (CTRL / CMD).
- Use the Convert Anchor Point Tool for ALT and OPTN+ Employ the Tool for Adding Anchor Points.
- Apply the tool to remove anchor points.

CREATING AND EDITING PATHS

The definition of path editing is as follows. Drawing a path on a painting with a pen, pencil, or curve tool involves drawing one or more straight or curved line segments. You can enhance and adjust a path to make any shape you can imagine or adjust its placement within the scene by using the Edit Path function. Shapes can be created in whatever way the object wishes. Click the Edit Path button after selecting the path to enter path editing mode.

Path types include:

- Open: A linked sequence of line segments in which the beginning and ending locations are not connected.
- Closed: A linked sequence of line segments in which a shape is formed by joining the start and end points.

WAYS TO CREAT AND CHANGE THE PATH

You must choose a path's segments, anchor points, or a mix of the two before you can alter or restructure it. To design a path, use the tools in the toolbar: Pen, Marker, and Bend

Let's start with the select anchor point:

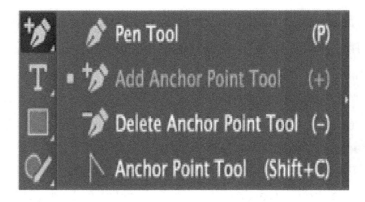

CHOOSE ANCHOR POINTS:

If the point is visible CHOOSE ANCHOR POINTS

To choose the points,

1. click on them using the Direct Selection tool if you can see them.
2. To choose more than one point, shift-click.
3. To create a border around the anchor points, select the Direct Selection tool and drag it.
4. To choose more anchor points, shift-drag around them. Anchor points from either the selected or unselected pathways can be chosen. After moving the Direct Selection tool over the anchor point until the cursor shows a filled square for paths that have been selected and a hollow square for unselected paths when zoomed, click the anchor point. To pick more anchor points, shift-click on them.

5. Choose the Lasso tool, then move it around the anchor points. To choose more anchor points, shift drag around them. ointments, press them

CHOOSE PATH SECTIONS

Choose the Direct Selection tool, then drag a marquee over a portion of the segment or click within two pixels of it. To pick other path segments, shift-click or shift-drag over them. Choose the Lasso tool and move a portion of the path segment around. To pick more path segments, shift-drag around them.

USING THE SHAPE BUILDER TOOL

To ensure that the forms and lines overlap or meet, know that the Shape Builder Tool only functions with closed paths before beginning.

To join numerous overlapping shapes, utilize the Shape Builder Tool. You can also subtract, merge, and erase forms in addition to that. Using it is really simple. Simply pick the forms and draw through them using the Shape Builder Tool. In Adobe Illustrator, the Shape Builder Tool is located on the toolbar and has the following appearance, in case you're wondering where it is.

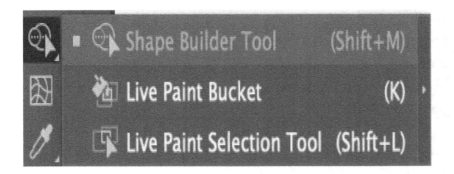

Shift + M is another keyboard shortcut that you can use to launch the Shape Builder Tool. Navigate to the left menu to utilize the Shape Tool. Click the tool's icon and select your preferred shape. After choosing the appropriate shape, click on the canvas and use the mouse to trace the shape.

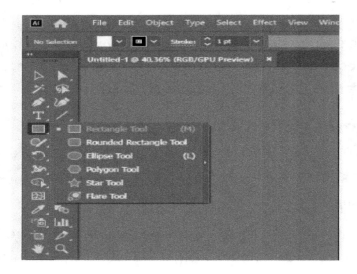

APPLYING STROKES AND FILLS

Adding colors, patterns, or gradients inside an object or on its outline is possible with the Fill and Stroke tool. Utilizing either the Selection or Direct Selection tools, choose the object. From the Toolbar, Properties, Control, or Color panels, select the Fill and Stroke tool. Click Fill twice to fill an object, and Stroke twice to create an outline. Your selection will be applied automatically to the selected object as soon as you make a selection from the Color panel at display.

NOTE: The color inside the shape is called the fill, and the visible outline of the object or path is called the stroke. It's crucial to know ahead of time whether you're trying to alter the fill or stroke color of the item that's currently chosen when you alter an icon's color. Then, make the appropriate toolbar selection.

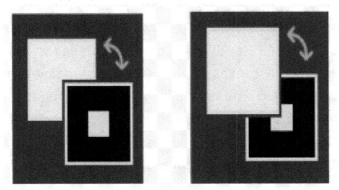

The first image has the fill color set to yellow, while the second image has the stroke color set to black. Clicking on any of the two will allow you to freely swap between them.

Use these steps to alter an object's color (fill or stroke):

1. Decide whatever item you wish to modify.
2. Depending on what you are trying to alter, click either the "fill" or the "stroke box", this will bring the "box" to the front (see image above).
3. To activate the color picker, click the box once more. Decide on the hue.
4. Press "OK."

UNDERSTANDING PATHFINDER OPERATIONS

Illustrator's Pathfinder tool manipulates specific paths and shapes. You can use it to build complex shapes, cut shapes into new forms, or combine numerous things into a single shape. It can combine, remove, intersect, or omit elements. With the help of this practical tool, you can easily modify various strokes and shapes to produce other, more complex ones. When you wish to merge multiple shapes, it comes in helpful.

HOW TO USE PATHFINDER OPERATION?

To launch Pathfinder, select Window, then Pathfinder from the Main Menu to make it visible. On PCs and Macs, you can also use the Shift + Cmd + F9 or Shift + Ctrl + F9 commands. Next, draw a new form on your canvas to gain an understanding of its various functionalities. You can use a simple design made up of two geometric forms or a more intricate pattern made up of many figures. While working with grouped elements, you may also utilize the tool to ungroup the figure elements to comprehend the functions.

In Illustrator, you must have at least two items selected in order to apply a pathfinder operation. Holding down the Shift key while clicking on various objects allows you to choose them.

The Operational Merit of Pathfinder:

1. The main benefit of pathfinder operations is that they give you a lot of freedom and control over the result.
2. The Pathfinder panel's options menu allows you to modify the parameters and settings of each operation;
3. The Align panel allows you to distribute or align your objects before executing a pathfinder operation.
4. The resultant shape can be changed into a compound path using the Expand command.

UTILIZING THE ALIGN AND DISTRIBUTE FUNCTIONS

ALIGNMENT OPTION:

You must select a minimum of two objects in order to align them. After that, you can select an alignment choice from the Align panel. As an illustration, you can align items to their boundaries, top, bottom, left, or right. The keyboard shortcuts Shift + F7, Shift + F8, and Shift + F9 can also be used to align left, center, and right, respectively. Once you have selected the other items, you may click on the key object (the one with the thicker outline) to align them to it.

NB: The Properties or Control panels also allow you to access them. You may distribute and align items to a key object, artboard, or selection, as well as horizontally and vertically. These panels facilitate this process. Along with aligning the objects to a pixel grid, you can also select the distance between each object.

DISTRIBUTION OPTION

You must pick at least three objects in order to distribute them. Next, you can select a distribution option from the Distribute menu. You can distribute items, for instance, by their edges or centers, either vertically or horizontally. By establishing a fixed value for the distance between items, you can also distribute them equally. To accomplish this, input the value in the Distribute Spacing field and select either the Vertical or Horizontal Distribute Space option.

How to distribute and align

Insertion of alignment and distribution tools;

1. Alignment modes The Align and Distribute tools' capability to alter the alignment mode is among its most helpful features. What the items are distributed or aligned to is determined by this. There are four options available to you: Align to Pixel Grid, Align to Artboard
2. Align to Selection, and Align to Key Object.
3. The alignment script Using scripts in Illustrator gives you more flexibility and control over how objects are aligned and distributed. Scripts are brief segments of code that carry out particular operations.

4. Using smart guides is an additional method in Illustrator for aligning and distributing objects. Temporary guides known as "smart guides" show up when you drag or resize items. They display the items' dimensions, alignment, and spacing with respect to one another.

CHAPTER 3

ADVANCED DRAWING AND EDITING

To elevate your artistic abilities to the next level, you can achieve advanced drawing by employing drawing techniques that go beyond the fundamentals. Advanced Drawing is intended to support an independent studio research course in an open studio setting.

Drawings can be broadly classified into two categories: technical and artistic. From the most basic line drawing to the most well-known paintings, artistic drawings come in many different forms. Artistic drawings, no matter how intricate, are meant to represent the artist's thoughts, feelings, and philosophies. Technical drawings, on the other hand, are typically used in conjunction with computerized CAD files to include details that are difficult to explain through part shape alone.

MASTERING THE CURVATURE TOOL

If you double-click the Curvature Tool, straight lines can also be created in addition to curved ones. As you design paths, you can modify them. The type tool and the conventional pen tool are on opposite sides of a single column toolbox that contains the curvature tool. Additionally, it can be accessed with the keyboard shortcut Shift+ Tilde. It should be noted that the tilde key is situated in the upper left corner on an American keyboard.

The Curvature tool

How to Use the curvature tool?

By automatically producing smooth curves between anchor points, the curvature tool makes the process of building curved routes easier. The tool uses the direction and distance of your mouse movement to compute and apply the curve when you click to add an anchor point. Click and drag on the anchor points or their handles to further modify the curvature.

To gain easy access, take the following step:

Select the "Curvature Pen Tool" from the list of available Pen Tools. The tool will automatically build curves linking the anchor points you click on on your canvas. To change the curvature, click and drag. Once you've sketched the appropriate form or path, keep adding anchor points and curves.

Using the Curvature tool to draw:

Select "new from template" from the file menu by clicking on it. Next, find your RGB file with center guidelines and open it to start a new document without a title. Here, in a single column toolbox between the type tool and the conventional pen tool, is where you'll find the curvature tool. Additionally, Shift+ Tilde is a keyboard shortcut for it. Furthermore, the tilde key on an American keyboard is situated in the upper left corner, as you may remember. Given that the tools symbol has a vertical tilde of sorts, it also makes some sense as a keyboard shortcut. Additionally, once the tool has been chosen and added to the

document window, you're

How to utilize Photoshop's curvature tool

Photoshop's curvature tool makes it simple to draw curved and smooth routes. Use it by doing the following:

1. Select the Pen Tool from the toolbar when Photoshop is open.
2. Select the "Curvature Pen Tool" from the Pen Tool menu.
3. The tool will automatically build curves linking the anchor points you click on to create on your canvas. Drag and click to change the curve.
4. 4.After you've sketched the shape or path you want, keep adding anchor points and curves.

WORKING WITH COMPOUND PATHS

In Adobe Illustrator, a compound path is created when two or more shapes interact with one another in such a way that gaps appear where they overlap. In other words, a compound path is made up of two or more overlapping objects that have see-through areas where they overlap. A compound path combines two or more pathways or objects into a single path, functioning more like a grouped item. Nevertheless, it is not possible to alter individual objects within a compound path. Each object's shape can be altered, but not its appearance. The Layers Panel is where you may find compound pathways.

The Creation of Compound Paths

A compound path is one that has holes in it. A letter, like B or O, is automatically transformed into a compound path when it is translated into an outline.

1. **Compound paths are created by doing the following:** Sketch two or more forms. arrange the smaller shapes on top of the larger one, make sure you design one shape that is larger than the rest.

2. Using the Selection Tool, choose both objects (shapes or photos, if applicable).

3. Select Compound Path under Object, then in Illustrator, what is the distinction between compound forms and compound? You combine paths in a compound path, and they are then handled as a single path. The pathways may intersect in part or not at all. To specify how a compound path behaves at the overlaps, utilize the fill rules, also known as winding rules. Examining the layer's panel is what matters.

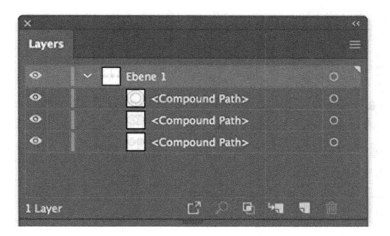

Compound forms are a more complicated type of object than compound paths, which are simply one entry in the layer's panel despite being nondestructive and yet releasable. Using the shape modes, the four uppermost buttons in the pathfinder panel, they can interact in various ways.

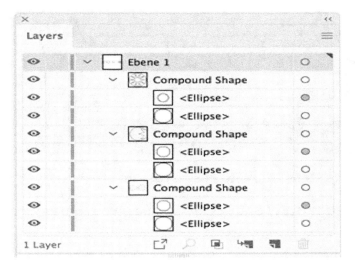

Note that while compound shapes are supported in certain other apps, they are primarily an Illustrator-only notion for real-time editing. In contrast, compound paths are a more universal vector graphic idea.

CREATING CUSTOM BRUSHES

There are only few brush possibilities in Adobe Illustrator. You have a simple, rounded-edge 3-point pen with a scratchy appearance that works well for lengthy strokes. These brushes aren't the only options available, though. Rather, they just allude to the various types of brushes you may create yourself, such as calligraphic, scatter, art, bristle, and pattern brushes.

Study the image below;

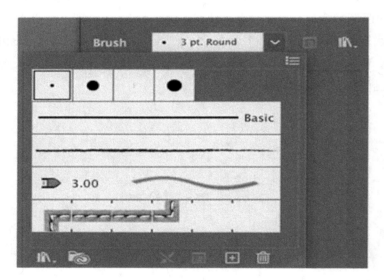

Follow the steps below to create custom brushes:

1. Select "NEW BRUSH" by tapping on the brushes panel.

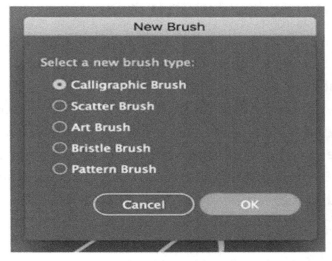

2. Click OK after entering the desired brush in the dialog box that displays.

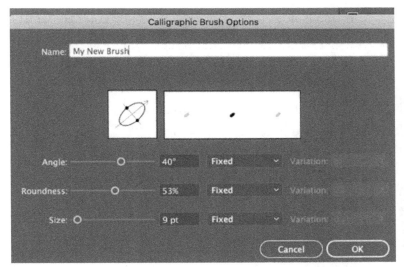

3. You can name the brush in the following dialog box (C). When the objects are placed on a path, there are choices to increase the distance between them or scale them.

USING THE BLOB BRUSH TOOL

Expanded brushstrokes can be created with Illustrator's Blob Brush Tool (Shift-B), which is why many designers use it for line drawings, character designs, or sketches. Brushes can be drawn as filled shapes using the Blob Brush Tool (Shift-B). Either choose this tool from the toolbar or hit the Shift-B keyboard shortcut to make it active. Expanded brushstrokes can be created with Illustrator's Blob Brush Tool (Shift-B), which is why many designers use it for line drawings, character designs, or sketches. Either choose this tool from the toolbar or hit the Shift-B keyboard shortcut to make it active.

How Is the Blob Brush Tool Used?

1. To create a brushstroke, make sure the Blob Brush Tool (Shift-B) is activated. Then, select and drag. The larger brush is added to your design when you release the mouse.
2. Select "merge only with selection" from the dialogue box that appears.

Note that if you follow these instructions exactly, your screen will look like the one in the picture below.

Similar to the standard brush, the blob brush offers all of the same panel settings. A brush preset's angle, roundness, and size can be adjusted by double clicking on it.

What can you make with the blob brush tool?

You can construct filled, compound paths using the Blob Brush tool by pressing the Paintbrush tool in the Toolbar. The Blob Brush tool allows for the blending of newly painted shapes with pre-existing shapes that have the same appearance parameters.

Employing brushes to apply a fill color:

A fill color can be applied to paint an object's interior when you use a brush to apply paint to its stroke. In areas where the fill and the brush objects overlap when you apply a fill color with a brush, the brush objects become visible above the fill color.

MANIPULATING OBJECTS WITH TRANSFORM TOOLS

Using the transform tool allows you to change an object's actual state. For proportionate resizing, shift-drag the handle of a bounding box. Click and drag to resize proportionately from the center by pressing Option+Shift (MacOS) or Alt+Shift (Windows). To turn an ellipse, drag the pointer away from the handle of a bounding box until the Rotate symbol appears. After that, drag to turn.

In Adobe Illustrator, how can I change an object's shape?

Use the Transform tool and proceed as follows:

1. Choose every item you wish to scale.
2. Use the shortcut command + option + shift + D, or select Object Transform each.
3. You have the option to rotate the items at a specified angle, scale them, and move them horizontally or vertically in the dialog box that appears.

APPLYING EFFECTS AND FILTERS

To create and isolate changes in a design layer, Adobe Illustrator makes use of filters and effects. These are comparable to photography filters in that you may use them to stylize photos to make them appear more traditional or illustrated.

When a filter is applied, the path's underlying structure is changed. Although Illustrator effects and filters are similar and sometimes use the same phraseology, filters are a more permanent change to the design that automatically changes the form of the design. Filters include adding fresco, film grain, poster extremes, and many other things. Illustrator has moved all of the features from the Filter menu to the effects menu, which is where the effects display on the appearance panel. Filters record permanent changes to the craft; they are destructive changes because you cannot undo the effects after saving and closing the file. effect merely modifies the path's look.

How Can I Use Illustrator's Filters?

a) Open your computer and launch Adobe Illustrator. Put a drawing or some text on the dashboard. We're going to use a text example here.

b) To apply a filter to an object or group of objects, use your Select tool to select them. The tools panel on the left-hand side contains the select tool.

EXPLORING THE APPEARANCE PAN

All changes made to a specific object are listed and made in the Appearance panel. You may adjust attributes like fill, stroke, blending mode, and opacity in the Appearance window. You may also regulate the effects that are applied to things with it. The Properties panel and the control bar additionally contain additional properties in addition to the fill and stroke colors. The most extensive control over item properties is available through the Appearance panel. You can view the fills, strokes, graphic styles, and effects that have been applied to an object, group, or layer using the Appearance Panel.

In Illustrator, how can I get to the Appearance panel?
In Illustrator, you can choose "Appearance" from the "Window" menu to open the Appearance panel. You can then adjust the appearance properties of the chosen objects by bringing up the

Appearance pane

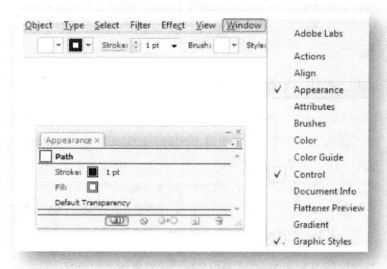

Note: When navigating through the Appearance palette, make sure that an object is chosen. The contents of the most recent object selected are displayed in this panel when it is empty, but editing it has no effect.

CHAPTER 4

TYPOGRAPHY AND TEXT EFFECTS

Making language visible through type arrangement is the art and skill known as typography. The word "typography" means "to arrange" and has Greek roots. Typography can be altered to create text effects, which enhance the readability of the information. It is a technique that modifies typeface appearance and highlights the meaning being expressed in words.

When should text effects be used?

Text effects work well in practically any design style, so you may apply them in a range of contexts. So that people would notice the extra effects and be impressed by your design, you want to employ it properly and tastefully. To ensure that text effects and typography don't overpower the other design elements, it's important to employ them as an accent or callback without going overboard.

What kind of text effect do we have?

Simple text effects include things like bold, italic, strikethrough, underlining, glow, gradient, embossing, and outline.

You can give characters a distinctive flair in Microsoft Word by using the Text Effects and Typography function.

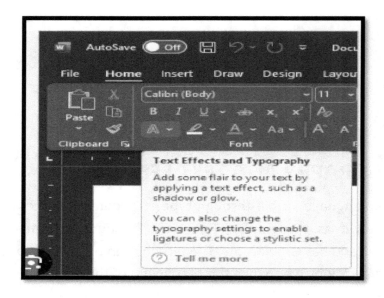

What kinds of results can you have with writing?

Typical writer's tropes include symbolism, foreshadowing, irony, strong imagery, and a variety of narrative vantage points. These effects can transmit deeper meanings, arouse feelings, build tension, and influence the writing's overall impact.

ADDING TEXT TO YOUR DESIGNS

Since you have to work with text in Adobe Illustrator for your design work 99.9% of the time, working with text is a major component of the workflow for graphic artists. In certain cases, all you might need to do is add a title; in other cases, you might need to design posters, logos, brochures, posters, and even your portfolio.

Move the pointer into text by selecting the Type tool. To pick a text, drag it over the screen. Modify text formatting options, including font size and family, in the Properties panel located to the right of the document. To view a list of Adobe typefaces, click Find More after choosing a font from the Font Family menu.

Follow the steps below to add text to your design

1. All you have to do is select the Type Tool (by pressing the T keyboard shortcut), copy and paste the text, then style it. After that, you can use the text to make logos, infographics, or whatever else you like.

2. Select your artwork by clicking on it. A selection of random text will be displayed to you.

It will display above.

3. Type your text in and double-click the text to erase it. Here, I put "MAY."

This approach works well for names, logos, and short texts because it's quick and simple to scale. When scaling to maintain the same shape, don't forget to hold down the Shift key.

FORMATTING TEXT ATTRIBUTES

Everything related to a particular character or set of characters' font, style, alignment, and other formatting is referred to as "text attributes".

Formatting, styling, and various operations such as word spacing, alignment, justification, and text transformation are all accomplished with the help of the text formatting attributes.

What is document formatting?

The visual arrangement and arrangement of a document on a page, including font selection, size, and presentation (bold or italic), spacing, margins, alignment, columns,indentation, and lists, are all considered aspects of document formatting.

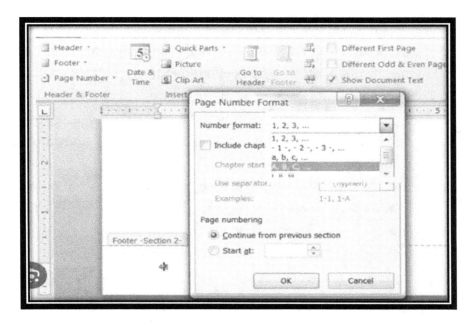

Text Formatting Properties:

The following are the attributes of text formatting:

1. Text-decoration: Text content can be "decorated" with the text-decoration attribute.

2. Text Color: You can set the text's color with this property. The color can be named "red," have a hex value of "#ff0000," or have an RGB value of "rgb (255,0,0)";

3. Text-align: This CSS property allows you to define the text's horizontal alignment inside a block element or table-cell box.

4. text-align-last: This style puts the paragraph's final line immediately before the line break. It aligns every last line that appears in the element that has the text align-last attribute applied to it.

5. text-decoration-color: This property controls the color of the decorations (throughs, underlines, and over lines) that are placed on top of the text.

6. Text-decoration-line: This is the line that sets the different types of text decorations. Values, such underline, over line, line-through, etc. may be included in this.

7. Text-decoration-style: The element's text-decoration can be adjusted using this property. It consists of the text-decoration-color and text-decoration-line attributes combined.

8. text-indent: This style, whose size might be in points, centimeters, or pixels, is used to indent the paragraph's first line.

9. text-justify: Text-align can be changed to justify using this attribute. The words are spread out into whole lines.

10. text-overflow: This formatting attribute indicates that a portion of the text has overflown and is

11. concealed from view.

12. text-transform: This command regulates the text's capitalization.

13. text-shadow: this property is used to give text a shadow.

14. letter-spacing: This attribute lets you define how much space there is between text characters.

15. Line-height: This property controls the distance between lines.

16. directions: The text's direction can be adjusted with this property.

17. Word-spacing: This specifies the distance in pixels between each word in a line.

CREATING TEXT ON A PATH

A type of artistic text known as "path text" traces the contours, lines, or curves of an object. Before and after path text conversion (as well as the finished design example). You can experiment with a wide variety of unique typographic designs by adding text to a path.

How to put text on a path in Illustrator?

How to Use Illustrator to Type on a Path
1. Using the Ellipse tool, draw a circle while holding down the Shift key.
2. Choose the Type on a Path Tool from the Text tool drop-down menu.
3. Click Window > Type > Paragraph to open the Type window and choose Paragraph.
4. Press the circle's upper center.

How to fit text to path in Illustrator?

Type on a Path Tool

1. Select the Ellipse Tool (keyboard shortcut L) from the toolbar. Hold the Shift key to make a perfect circle.
2. Select the Type on a Path Tool.
3. Replace the Lorem Ipsum with your own text.
4. Align to Path controls the distance of the text to the path.

Creating text in a curved route:

1. Start the Illustrator project.
2. Use the toolbar on your left to find the ellipse tool.
3. Use the tool to draw a circle.
4. Next, select the "Text" tool from your toolbar. Fifth, choose the "Type On A Path Tool."
5. Click the circle where you just made the path.

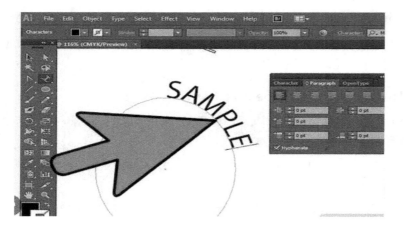

The diagram above illustrates how to create text on a path.

APPLYING TEXT EFFECTS

Text can be enhanced with an effect. if you truly like to use fancy text formatting. With the addition of an outline, shadow, reflection, or glow to your text, you can create new designs or alter the fifteen pre-existing ones. Experimentation is the greatest approach to feel comfortable using text effects. Using a larger font size frequently improves the visibility of text effects.

Click Text Effect in the Font group on the Home tab. To add an effect, click on it.

What is an example of a text effect?

Within the Font group on the Home tab, select Text Effect. Click on the effect you wish to add.

Note: To give characters a distinct look, use Microsoft Word's Text Effects and Typography tool.

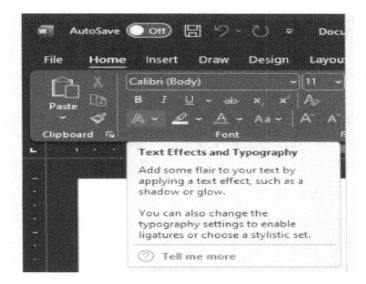

Text effect display;

Use a Text Effect

1. Decide the text you wish to have a text effect applied to it. Word accentuates the text.
2. In the Font group, select the Text Effect button.
3. Select the desired effect. Word applies your chosen effect.

Press the text field. The underlining vanishes.

1. Put on a Glow, Shadow, or Mirror:

    1. Pick out the text that you wish to add a text effect on.
2. Select the Font group and click the Text Effect button. Select either Glow, Shadow, or Reflection.
3. Select the desired effect to use.

To eliminate an effect, select No Glow, No Reflection, or No Shadow. To apply different effects, such as outline weight, outline style, or color, click on the same steps as for "apply effect," changing only the effect you are now using, such as "apply outline style."

WORKING WITH PARAGRAPH STYLES

A paragraph style is a collection of characteristics that define the appearance of the text within a paragraph, such as the font size and color.

Character and paragraph formatting elements are both included in a paragraph style. It can be used on a single paragraph or a group of paragraphs.

What are styles?

Style is the way something is spoken or done, and it is distinct from the meaning or content that it contains.

What are character styles and paragraph styles?

A character style is an assembly of formatting properties for characters that can be used to format text in a single step. A paragraph style can be applied to a single paragraph or a group of paragraphs, and it contains formatting and character properties. Character styles and paragraph styles are located on different panels. Text styles are another name for paragraph and character s tyles. Any text to which a style has been applied will be updated with the new format whenever you make changes to the style's formatting.

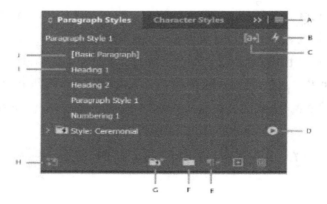

To quickly create a new Character or Paragraph style, simply follow these steps:

- Pick a text.
- To view the Paragraph styles panel, select Type > Paragraph styles.
- To build a style using the chosen text format, click build a New Style.

Why are paragraph styles important?

It is much more than only body paragraphs that can use paragraph styles. Headings, lists, quotations, sidebars, and more can all benefit from the use of paragraph styles. Formatting for a paragraph is applied across all paragraph styles.

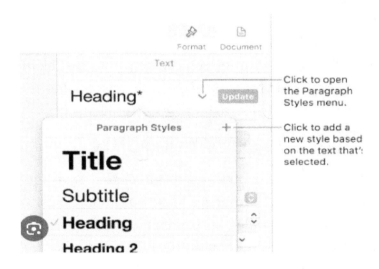

Illustrating introduction to paragraph style.

UTILIZING TYPE ON A PATH OPTIONS

By using Adobe Illustrator's "Type on a Path" feature, you can add a unique and dynamic touch to your designs by creating type that follows a specific route or form.

The following provides a thorough guide on utilizing this feature: Using the Ellipse tool, draw a circle while holding down the Shift key.

1. Choose the Type on a Path Tool from the Text tool drop-down menu.
2. Click Window > Type > Paragraph to open the Type window and choose Paragraph. As an alternative, select the Panel Options and click the Align Center option.
3. Press the circle's upper center. An input cursor that flashes appears.
4. Text entered is centered and aligned as you type. Click the Character tab while the Type panel is open. Enter the text for the circle's top after selecting a font and size.
5. Use the Symbols palette to select an appropriate symbol and drag it to adjust its size.

Using the "Type on a Path" option can help your text elements stand out and draw in readers by bringing in an additional layer of inventiveness and visual intrigue to your designs.

IMPORTING AND EXPORTING FONTS

Documents, photos, and other digital goods that have been moved from one program to another are known as import files. Importing a file entails downloading it from an external source onto a platform. The currently running software must identify and decode the file before it can be used. Import Fonts can be selected by right-clicking on Fonts. A window in File Explorer appears locally. Add a font import to particular channels.

Your image can be exported to be saved in a variety of file formats, including JPEG, PNG, PDF, and EPS. Using Illustrator's Export or Save for Web features is required in order to export an image.

What does font import and export mean?

Bringing a file into a program is called import. It could involve adding to a database or opening a file. The process of exporting a file from one program to another involves saving it in a different format (which is essentially a copy of the original file) and frequently for use in a different software.

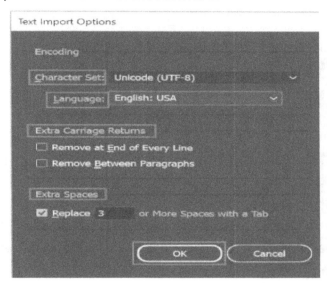

Text import option display.

Text import capability are as follows:

1. Indicate the character set and language were used to produce the file.
2. To see how Illustrator handles extra carriage returns in the file, select Extra Carriage Returns.
3. To instruct Illustrator to insert tabs in place of space characters across the project, select Extra Spaces. To have a tab substitute a space, provide its number.

Import text into a new file

To import text into new file, do the following:

- Click on File > Open.
- Click on Open after choosing the text file you wish to see.
- After making your changes, click OK to close the Text Import Options dialog box.

Import text into an existing file:

- Select File > Location.
- Choose Place after selecting the text file you wish to import.
- If the file is a plain text (.txt), adjust the options in the Text Import Options dialog box and click OK.

Exporting text

In Illustrator, how can fonts be exported? Simply select the file type you want to develop under File > Generate in order to export your unique font. True Type Format, or TTF, is the most widely used. You should load and test your Typeface in your font application after you've exported it. All of the characteristics of text can be exported from Illustrator as a text file.

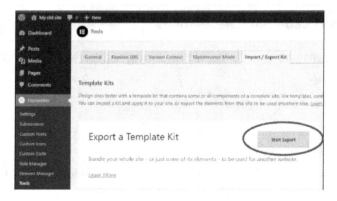

Steps to export practically:
- Choose the text you wish to export using a Type tool.

- Select File > Export > Export As, give the file a location, and type a filename.
- Select Text Format (.TXT) as the format for the file.
- Type the new text file's name into the name box, then choose Export (macOS) or Save (Windows).
- Click Export after selecting a platform and an encoding technique.

Text export diagram.

CHAPTER 5

WORKING WITH COLORS AND GRADIENTS

Determining which colors go well together is done through a practical application of science and art called "Working with Color." It has the ability to express emotions and moods. is employed, like stop signs or the yellow vs white directional stripes on roads, to bring order and organization to life.

A color harmony is created when two or more colors go well together. These are used by designers and artists to produce a specific style or mood. By applying the principles of color combinations, you can utilize a color wheel to identify color harmonies.

The seamless transition of one or more tones on our canvas is called a gradient. Gradients are typically used to create aesthetically pleasing and calming backdrops. It will draw attention to your text and give your designs more depth, which will make them stick out. However, while working with gradients, ensure that there is a seamless color transition and avoid going overboard. Generally, a color gradient is created by blending two or more colors together, but you can use any combination of colors to create a gradient. Gradients are a very fashionable design feature that can give your projects more visual intrigue and depth.

Sample of a gradient color

UNDERSTANDING COLOR MODES

To display colors uniformly across media and platforms, designers employ color modes. While they vary in quality and file size, commonly used modes include LAB, RGB, CMYK, index, grayscale, and bitmap. In order to maintain brand consistency, designers use modes that optimize images and guarantee that they appear unchanged across media.

Sorts of Color Modes

1. RGB (Red, Green, Blue): This color space is perfect for capturing and showing images with true-to-life color depth, as well as for digital interfaces like websites, applications, and games where brilliant colors stand out.

2. CMYK (Cyan, Magenta, Yellow, Key/Black): it works well for printed products, guarantees color uniformity and precision, and works well in brochures, magazines, and packaging.

3. LAB (Lightness; A for green-red axis, B for blue-yellow axis): This color perception chameleon is useful for multi-platform design websites, print, and packaging since it represents colors based on human vision. It also ensures color harmony.

4. Grayscale: this style is ideal for classic photography, artwork, and creating atmosphere or expressing timeless elegance since it emphasizes tone changes (from black to white).
5. Bitmap: a technique for creating images from individual colored pixels. For designs with a retro feel, it's crucial. Aesthetics of pixel art and nostalgia combined.

CREATING AND MANAGING SWATCHES

In Adobe Illustrator, color swatches are crucial tools for speed and uniformity. They lessen the need for manual color value entry by enabling you to save and reuse colors throughout your artwork, guaranteeing a unified color scheme.

Creating Color Swatches

To make swatches, follow these steps:

1. Choose the color: Utilize the eye dropper tool to identify the desired color from your piece of art.
2. Click on the window menu to choose which swatches to display in order to bring up the swatches panel.
3. To add color to swatches, drag the chosen color into the swatches panel or click the new swatch button in the swatches panel.
4. To rename the swatch, double-click on its name and enter the intended designated color.

Handling Color Swatches:
- Make a duplicate swatch by clicking and dragging it onto the Swatches panel using the "New Swatch" button.
- Delete Swatches: To remove a swatch from the Swatches window, select it and press the Delete key.

- Rearrange Swatches: To change the order of swatches, click and them across the Swatches panel.
- Swatches can be exported for use in other projects or imported from other Adobe Illustrator works.

Applying Solid Colors and Gradients

What do solid and gradient colors mean?
Solid fill evenly applies one color to an object's whole surface. With gradient fill, two or more colors are continuously blended together, with one hue progressively fading into another. If you align two anchor nodes in the same spot within the Color Gradient, you can create solid colors in the gradient fill.

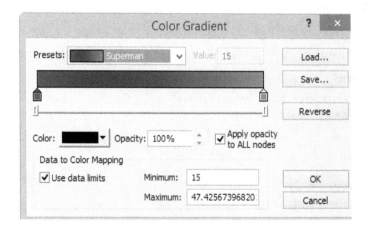

Color gradient form a superman preset.

You can use one of four sorts of solid colors:
1. Theme Colors are a collection of hues chosen to correspond with the current theme of your presentation.
2. The ten colors that other users use the most frequently make up Standard Color.
3. Other Used Colors is a collection of the colors you have most recently utilized.

4. You can customize the Advanced Color Palette to fit your brand and business by selecting from a variety of color schemes that are included.

Apply Gradient Colors

Selecting your gradient colors is similar to selecting your solid fill colors, but only for the areas of the slide that the gradient color you choose will be applied to.

1. On the gradient scale, choose the desired Start or Stop handle.
2. Select your preferred color by clicking the Color dropdown.

To add or remove a gradient point, take note:

o   Either click the Plus icon above the gradient scale or select a point on the scale. Move the points by dragging them over the scale.
o   To remove the chosen point, click the Minus icon.

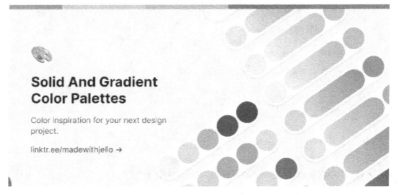

Diagram illustrating solid and gradient color

WORKING WITH LIVE PAINT

Using Live Paint to make colorful paintings is simple and straightforward. Although all of Illustrator's vector drawing tools are available to you, all of the paths you draw are treated as though they are on a single, flat surface. In other words, none of the pathways are in front of or behind another. Instead, regardless of whether an area is bounded by a single path or by segments of numerous paths, the paths divide the drawing surface up into areas that can all be colored. As a result, painting something is similar to coloring in a coloring book or adding watercolors to a pencil drawing.

Edges and faces are what you can paint on Live Paint groups. A path's edge is the section that separates its intersections with other paths. A face is a region that has one or more edges surrounding it. Faces and edges can be filled and stroked.

What is the shortcut for live paint in Illustrator?

After selecting your drawing, navigate to the Shape Builder tool in your toolbar, drag the menu out, and choose Live Paint Bucket (keyboard shortcut: K).

How does live paint work?

You can add color to regions using Live Paint even if they are not closed shapes. You can apply colors to sections or strokes using the Live Paintbrush or Live Paint Bucket tools by first drawing shapes and then converting them to Live Paint Objects.

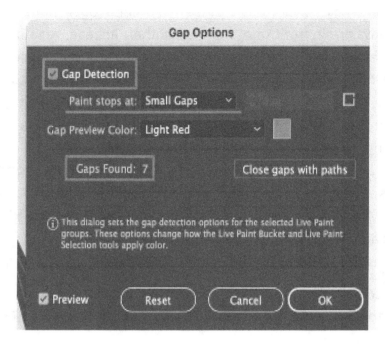

Live paint bucket display.

How Can I Apply the Paint Bucket Tool Live?

Take the actions listed below:

1. Select the area or items to be colored with the Live Paint Bucket tool by using the Selection Tool (keyboard shortcut V).

2. With the items selected, select Object from the overhead toolbar. From the expanded menu, choose Live Paint and then select Make. The items will become Live Paint Groups as a result.

3. To use the Live Paint Bucket tool, either select it from the left toolbar or use the shortcut key (K).

4. Select the color from the color swatches that you want to use throughout your artwork.

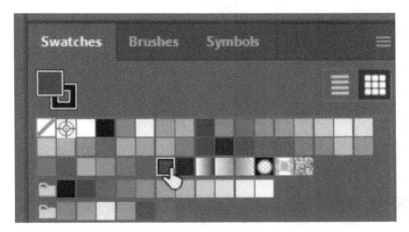

5. Choose the hue you wish to use all over your artwork from the color swatches.

USING THE RECOLOR ARTWORK FEATURE

I wish more people will use Recolor Artwork because it's both a lifesaver and a lot of fun. The best part about Recolor Artwork is that, once you figure it out, you can rapidly give your artwork a color makeover. You also won't need to scroll through endless Pinterest images to realize that, in order to make your work truly stand out, it is essential to have an eye-catching color palette.

RECOLOR ARTWORK TOOL:

- Open Adobe Illustrator and develop a new color scheme for your work.
- After choosing your new color scheme, select Object > Group.
- After choosing your piece of art, select Edit > Edit Colors > Recolor Artwork.
- Select your new color scheme by clicking on the Color Theme Picker.

How to recolour an image?

How to alter an image's color:

- Start using Canva. To use our free online photo editor, open the Canva app on your phone or in your browser.
- Put your photo online. Drag and drop the desired image onto the canvas after uploading it.
- Adjust the image's color scheme.
- Apply the final details.
- Save and distribute.

EXPLORING GLOBAL COLORS

Colors are an effective tool that have a big effect on the user experience. They have the power to strengthen emotional ties inside a design, affecting the emotions and actions of people. This article will examine the basic ideas of color theory as well as the significance of colors in the context of user experience. With Illustrator, you may quickly alter the color of every object by using the global colors setting. It associates the color with a swatch in

Illustrator's Swatches panel, so that any changes you make to the swatch will also update all objects that use that color.

How do you make a global color?

Double-clicking a swatch in the Swatches panel and selecting Global from the Swatch Options dialog box will make it global. Place a white triangle in the corner to represent Global Swatches. Have a single tint slider in the Color Panel so you may adjust the color's brightness. Changing a color in the swatch panel is simple with global colors; the changes are reflected throughout the document where the swatch is used. This allows for quick and simple testing of the appearance of a color shift in a matter of seconds.

INCORPORATING COLOR GROUPS AND LIBRARIES

To successfully manage and utilize colors in graphic design, digital art, and branding, color groups and libraries are incorporated into the design process techniques.

Here's a detailed explanation:

Color Groups:

A grouping of colors with a same theme, style, or palette is called a color group. It's a method for grouping colors into relevant categories so that they can be more easily accessed and used consistently throughout designs.

One way to categorize colors is by:
1. brand identification (main, secondary, and accent colors, for example).
2. Design aesthetic (bold, monochrome, or pastel, for example)
3. Tone of emotion (warm, chilly, or neutral, for example)
4. Sector or subject (such as technology, healthcare, or the environment)

Color Libraries:

A color library is an easily accessible and organized collection of colors that are frequently kept as swatches

Color libraries can take the following forms or color references that can be used in designs:

- Hard copy swatch books or color cards
- Digital files (such as Adobe Color, Sketch, or Sigma files).
- Websites or online color databases.

Take the following actions to incorporate color libraries and groups into your design process:

1. Create color groups: Based on your design requirements, define and group your colors into meaningful ways.
2. Create a color library: Put your color groupings in a physical or digital library that is centrally located.
3. Use color libraries in your designs: To maintain consistency between designs, access and apply colors from your library.
4. Refine and update: To reflect modifications to your design aesthetic or brand identification, periodically examine and update your color collection.
5. Collaborate and share: To guarantee color consistency between projects, share your color library with clients or team members.

Following these steps will let you include color libraries and groups into your design process:

1. Form meaningful color groups: Depending on the requirements of your design, define and group your colors into appropriate categories.
2. Create a color library. You can save your color groups physically or digitally in a centralized library.

3. Use color palettes in your designs: To guarantee consistency between designs, access and utilize colors from your palette.
4. Review and update often: To accommodate modifications to your design aesthetic or brand identification, make sure your color collection is up to date.
5. Share and work together: To guarantee color coherence across projects, share your color library with clients or team members.

Designers can assure color consistency, expedite workflow, and produce visually appealing designs that successfully convey their message by arranging and employing color groups and libraries.

CHAPTER 6

ADVANCED TECHNIQUES FOR ILLUSTRATION

One kind of visual representation of written content is an illustration. They could serve as ornamentation, a means of illustrating a point, or both. They are produced in a range of media, including digital and conventional.

The styles and techniques used in illustration are very diverse and include digital design, multimedia, 3D modeling, printmaking, collage, montage, and sketching. Illustrations can be very technical, realistic, expressive, or stylized, depending on their intended use.
There are two types of illustration techniques: conventional and modern. In the past, artists mainly used paper, paints, and pencils. However, as the digital era developed, a lot of illustrators started working digitally.

The following are techniques for illustrations:

1. Pencil illustrations: Pencils are a sophisticated media that enable you to create fine lines and precise shadows and transitions.
2. Charcoal illustrations are perfect for short narrative and quick sketches. Artists frequently blend, smear, and create delicate shadowing with their fingers and tissues. Using oil, lard, or wax, lithography is a method that creates an image on the surface of a level, flat lithographic limestone plate.
3. Watercolor pictures Color pigments and water are used in watercolor drawings to create nuances and a range of transparency.

4. Since acrylic paint is simpler to use than water-or oil-based paints, it is one of the most widely used methods for novice illustrators.

There are many more illustration approaches, these are just a select selection.

DRAWING AND EDITING CUSTOM ARTWORK

What is custom art?

The artist creates CUSTOM ARTS specifically for you based on your requests. He or she uses your own concept in this instance. You can give the artist a detailed description of your idea or just a general idea with creative freedom. Additionally, you can request a particular style that you like.

What is the appropriate fee for a personalized illustration?
In an 11" x 17" drawing, multiply the width by the height to find the number of square inches. 11, 17 = 187 square inches. The price per square inch, or $4.20, is what we'll round that down to. In light of this, I would price $336 for an original 8" by 10".

Custom art provides a customized expression that fits the goals and requirements of the customer, in contrast to mass-produced art. Along with working directly with the artist to realize their vision, it also enables clients to participate in the creative process.

A custom design is an original and customized design made to satisfy the needs and desires of a customer. It reflects their vision, brand identity, and preferred aesthetic and is customized to meet their demands.

USING THE IMAGE TRACE TOOLS

In Illustrator, how can I use image trace?

1. 1.Choose Window > Image Trace in Adobe Illustrator while the image is open.
2. Check the Preview box while the image is selected.
3. Choose the mode that best fits your design by selecting it from the Mode drop-down menu.
4. After that, modify the sliders for colors, grays, or threshold.
5. **How Can I Use Illustrator to Make a Background Transparent?**
   - Click on Your Picture: In the event that the file already exists, select "File," find your photo, and click "Open.
   - Examine Your Options
   - Turn on the Grid of Transparency.
   - Modify as necessary
   - Keep Your Photo Safe
   - Check for transparency
   - Launch Illustrator, Include or Produce an Image

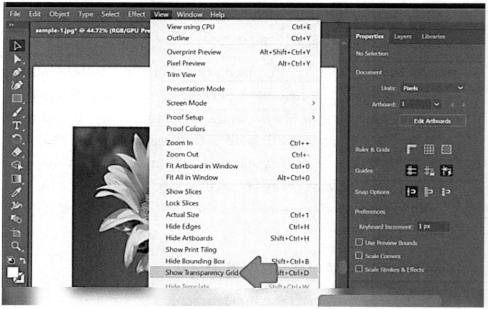

Where in Illustrator is Image Trace located?

Drag and drop a raster image onto your Artboard from an Adobe Illustrator file. To trace the image using preset parameters, select it and go to Object > Image Trace > Make.

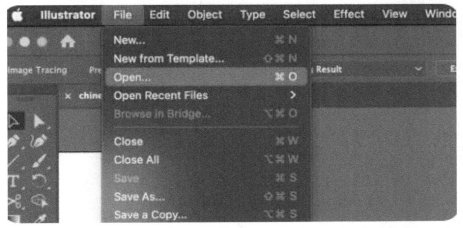

Locate the image by clicking on "open " as shown in the diagram. It will direct you to your files. From the dropdown list , click 'image trace.

How to trace image In Illustrator, how can I make an image outline?

- Click on the Pen Tool.
- From the toolbar, select the Pen Tool (P).
- Set Stroke Color and Weight: For your outline, decide on the stroke color and weight.
- These can be adjusted in the Stroke or Control panels.

Using Image Trace, remove the background in Illustrator; Select "Windows" and then "Image Trace" from the pop-up menu that appears. In the newly opened pop-up window, you can adjust the settings as necessary. To eliminate the backdrop from an image, pick "Color" after adjusting the mode and determine how many colors to use.

CREATING 3D OBJECTS

With the use of 3D effects, two-dimensional (2D) artwork can be transformed into three-dimensional (3D) things. 3D objects have attributes like lighting, shading, rotation, and others that allow you to alter how they seem. Additionally, you can overlay artwork onto every surface of a three-dimensional object.

Revolving or extruding are the two methods available for creating 3D objects.

Extrude to make a 3D object:

To give a 2D item more depth, extrusion involves extending the object along its z axis. A 2D ellipse, for instance, becomes a cylinder when it is extruded.

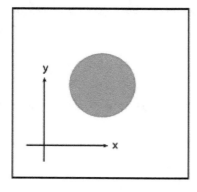 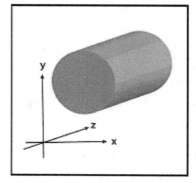

Turn a thing into a three-dimensional object by rotating:

To generate a three-dimensional object, revolving involves sweeping a route or profile in a circular motion around the global y axis, also known as the rotate axis. As a result of the revolve axis' vertical fixation, the open or closed route you revolve usually has to show half of the required 3D object's profile in a front-facing, vertical position. After that, you can rotate the 3D object's location using the effect's dialog box.

WORKING WITH PERSPECTIVE GRIDS

An illustration framework known as a perspective grid consists of a horizon line, which is a horizontal line that depicts your field of vision, orthogonal grid lines, which are lines that "vanish" into a focal point, at least one vanishing point, which is the point on the horizon line where all lines converge, and at least one appropriate plane.

By using the Perspective Grid Tool (Shift+p), one can manipulate the grid's planes, cell size, and other features without compromising the artwork. When rearranging shapes on the grid, the Perspective Selection Tool (Shift+v) allows you to interact with them while maintaining their perspective.

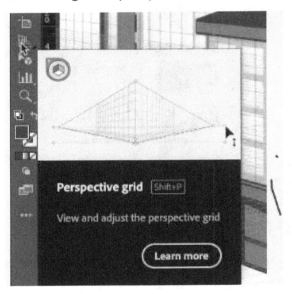

Using perspective grid in illustrator.

How does Illustrator's grid tool work? Grids can be created with the Rectangular Grid tool.

1. click the tool for Rectangular Grid.

2. Use your mouse to draw a rectangle grid on the artboard
3. Press and hold the Rectangular Grid tool to bring up the Rectangular Grid Tool Options window.
4. Double-click and drag the path using the Selection tool to modify the pathways in the grid.

In the perspective grid, how do you add an object? The Perspective Selection tool allows you to drag and drop an object into the desired spot on the perspective grid. To adjust the Perspective Grid Options dialog box and change the tool's parameters, double-click the Perspective Selection tool.

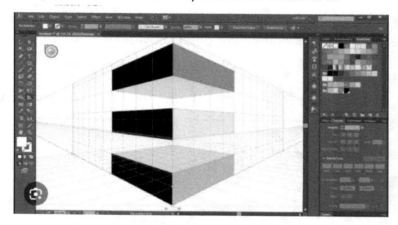

How to use the perspective grid

APPLYING MASKS AND CLIPPING PATHS

The visibility of vector objects can be controlled based on another item using both masks and clipping paths. An object that determines the opacity of the items beneath it is called a mask, and an object that defines the form of the objects inside it is called a clipping path. For instance, a clipping path can be used to remove a picture inside a circle, or a mask can be used to provide a gradient effect on text.

An item or group is more transparent when it is darker than the masking object. Using the keyboard shortcuts Ctrl+7 (Windows) or Command+7 (Mac), select both objects and click Object > Clipping Mask > Make to create a mask. Double-clicking on a mask or selecting Object > Clipping Mask > Edit or Release will allow you to change or release it.

The advantages of clipping paths and masks

1. There are various advantages to masks and clipping paths in vector art.
2. You can use them to make intricate compositions without changing the original elements.
3. It maintains their scalability and edit ability. Moreover, they maximize performance and reduce file size.
4. They cut down on how many points and pathways are displayed. They give you the ability to simultaneously apply transformations and effects, including filters and shadows, to several objects.

Masks and clipping disadvantages.

For vector art, there are certain restrictions and difficulties with masks and clipping paths.

1. They can be challenging to understand and handle, particularly if you have a lot of levels and nested objects.
2. Additionally, they may result in unanticipated outcomes or mistakes, such as masks not appearing in some export formats or clipping masks not working with gradient meshes.
3. They could result in your artwork losing some of its intricacies or colors, or in jagged edges or gaps that detract from its overall quality.

INTEGRATING SYMBOLS AND SYMBOL LIBRARIES

Just picture having a vast collection of reusable graphic elements at your disposal, just ready to be discovered and used in your creations. The secret to finding this treasure lies in symbol libraries and symbols themselves, which let you add coherence, consistency, and a splash of artistic flair to your artwork.

It's like unleashing a creative tempest when you use symbols and symbol libraries into your design workflow. This revolutionary tool enhances efficiency, reduces waiting times, and allows you to concentrate on the creative process of design instead of having to start from scratch.

Explore the realm of symbols and symbol collections to fully appreciate the impact of visual narratives.

What is the meaning of symbols?

What is meant to be represented by a sign, shape, or item is called a symbol. To designate something, a symbol can be any character, mark, letter, number, or combination of characters.

What is symbol & library?

A library of symbols is a collection of symbols. Generally, the symbols found in a symbol library are either part of a certain set or align with a particular standard. Libraries of symbols can be kept in a master data pool or a project.

How do I create a symbol library?

Establishing Symbol Libraries

To establish symbol and libraries, follow the steps below:

- Choose the subsequent menu items: Tools > Master information > Symbol library > New.

- From the Save in drop-down list in the Create symbol library dialog, choose a drive and a directory to save the new symbol library to.
- Replace the default file name with "New symbol library."

Advantage of combining symbol libraries and symbols

a. If you have a large number of symbols, Symbol Libraries can help you manage and arrange them.
b. Equations and data can be made more succinct and concise by using symbols.
c. Scientists find symbols useful as performing their work by hand would need time and paper.

ENHANCING ILLUSTRATIONS WITH BLENDS AND PATTERNS

In Illustrator, what do blends mean? Object color and repeating form creation are possible with Illustrator's blend tool. This tool gives you the option to blend two open paths to provide a seamless transition between objects or to blend objects and colors together to produce color transitions within the contour of the object.

How can I use Illustrator to combine patterns?

Holding Shift will allow you to use the Selection tool to choose the first and second lines. In order to build the pattern, select Object > Blend > Make. After that, double-click the Blend tool to adjust the Blend Options to the values indicated in the picture. Continue blending.

Keep in mind that harmony, pattern, and blend can turn your drawings into engrossing pieces of art that convey feeling and make an impact.

Using blend tool to create pattern

CHAPTER 7

EXPORTING AND OUTPUTTING YOUR WORK

You must transfer your dataset from OpenRefine to the system of your choosing as soon as it is available. OpenRefine can generate or edit statements on Wikidata, export files in a variety of file formats, and upload data straight into Google Sheets.

Additionally, you have the option to export your entire project data so that it may be opened with OpenRefine by another person or by you on an other computer.

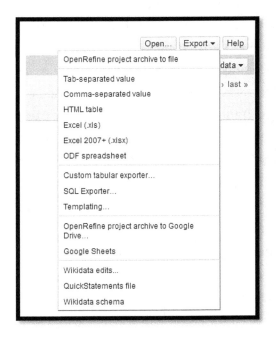

Select the desired format by clicking the Export dropdown menu located in the upper right corner of a project to export data in that format.

The choices you have are:

1. The values separated by a tab (TSV) or comma (CSV)
2. Table formatted in HTML
3. Open Document Format (ODF) spreadsheet (ODS) Excel spreadsheet (XLS or XLSX
4. Upload to Google Sheets

Is it possible to export specific PDFs from Illustrator?

To do so, take the following actions:

a) Verify that PDF is chosen in the Format Dropdown. This will enable the Single File or Multiple Files 'Export PDF as options to be clickable.

b) Choose More Than One File. c) Select which artboards to export by using the checkmarks.

How to Export an Illustrator or InDesign Print-Ready PDF File

You should make sure your design file is print-ready before exporting it. Having a little refresher on the details is always beneficial, regardless of your level of experience or how long it has been since you had to prepare a file for printing. Thus, all the information you require to ensure that your drawings are printed at the appropriate quality before exporting is provided below.

Prior to exporting a file, quickly make sure that:

a. The Bleed Area is fully filled with your background content

b. There are no important content outside the Safety Margin

c. Double-check your spelling and any design-related errors

d. Remove any objects from the artboard that are not intended to be printed, including any extra layers, swatches, links, or extra objects

e. Check links that are missing or that need to be updated

f. Make sure that the document color mode is set to CMYK
g. Make sure that the images are at least 300 dpi
h. Outline your text to prevent font-related problems; Delete any templates you used, or at least make that layer visible.

SAVING AND EXPORTING FILES

In order to open the active document with a different software, Export is typically used to create a fresh copy of it in a format that is not generally supported. The option to "Save As" allows you to make a fresh duplicate of the current document in a format that is often supported by the application (in this example, Word).

SAVE:

Preserving modifications in a format that the program can use directly means that the file format is maintained. Data formats are altered during exportation to enable use by another program. (For example, converts a PNG file to a JPG file).

A saved document is usually anticipated to be the same as the original (possibly with the exception of features not available in earlier file format versions). An exported document might differ from the original because the new format might not support the same feature set.

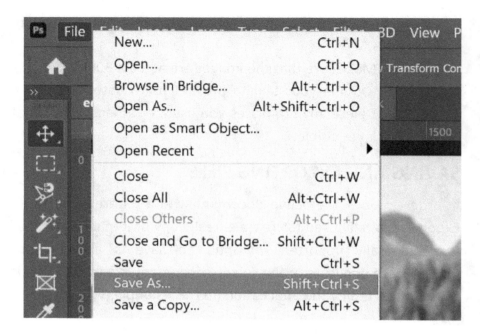

Image illustrating save as mode

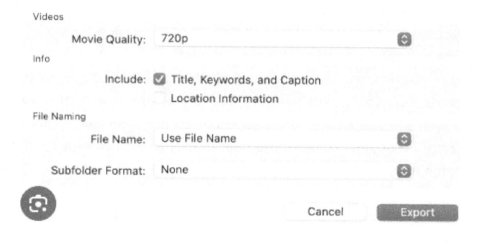

Exporting image

UNDERSTANDING FILE FORMATS

Comprehending file formats is essential as it facilitates the handling of diverse file formats and guarantees interoperability with various software and gadgets. You can find out which programs are needed to open, modify, or play a certain file by understanding its format. The arrangement of data inside a file is referred to as its format. It establishes the methods by which different software programs encode, store, and understand the data. For various uses, including text documents, photos, videos, audio files, and more, different file formats are created.

Which file formats are frequently used for text documents? Text document file types that are often used are:

- o TXT: Unformatted plain text files.
- o DOCX: Microsoft Word processing documents, which are commonly utilized.
- o Portable Document Format (PDF): This format is widely used to share read-only documents.
- o RTF: Rich Text Format, which works with a number of word processing programs.

What are some common audio file formats?

Frequently used audio file types are:

a) MP3 (MPEG Audio Layer-3), which is commonly utilized for compressed audio files.
b) WAV: Waveform Audio File Format, renowned for its high-quality, uncompressed audio.
c) Advanced Audio Coding (AAC) is frequently utilized on mobile devices and streaming services.
d) FLAC: Free Lossless Audio Codec, renowned for its high-quality audio and lossless compression.

Types of files

Variations in file formats can accomplish variations in subtitles and are compatible with various software. An RTF file or a standard text document cannot be used to add content to a video, however an

SRT file can be. Certain picture file formats work better for digital graphics than others, especially when it comes to printing.

We categorize files into four main types

Specifically: image, text, audio, and picture

Document   Image   Video   Audio

Using the appropriate file formats helps lower bounce rates and boost engagement whether developing a website or sending out marketing emails.

It is possible to gain an edge over your competitors by optimizing your online strategy and marketing campaign by selecting the appropriate file format.

Types of document files

A few distinct document formats exist, and each has unique advantages and formatting capabilities. The formats for document files are XLS and XLSX, HTML and HTM, PDF, and DOC and DOCX.

Types of image files

GIFs, JPEGs, and PNGs are among the most widely used formats for image files.

Types of video files

A few of the most common file formats for videos include MP4, AVI, and MOV. Videos are a fantastic method to interact with your audience.

Types of audio files

In the world of audio formats, MP3 may be the most well-known, but there is also M4A, MPEG, and Apple CREATED M4A for songs and the iTunes ecosystem.

PREPARING ARTWORK FOR PRINT

If you consider "Artwork" to be the general word for the layout file, that could be helpful. All the contents of the file are covered. Your printing firm is requesting the layout as a whole, not just the pictures or photos, if they want you to submit your artwork (which they may just call "Art").

The right file type, resolution, and dimensions for the finished output are what make an artwork print-ready. For printing to preserve clarity and detail, it needs to have all fonts and a DPI (Dots Per Inch) of 300 or above.

Easy Steps for Producing Art that Is Print-Ready

a. Pick a format for the file. Generally, PDF works best.

b. Include a bleed zone. A bleed area of 2 to 4 millimeters is needed for most printing.

b) Transform to vector pathways or embed every typeface. Using the CMYK color standard, save your artwork as a single-layered picture.

What are printable art supplies?

Essential Resources:

- Bradley Ink for printing (at least two colors, of your choice)
- Tray for ink.
- A single EZ Carve or linoleum block, in any size
- U and V tips for a vinyl cutter.

Kindly take note that if you lack many of the supplies mentioned above, you can save money by getting the Speedball Printmaking Starter Kit.

How should artwork be sent to be printed?

a. Fit the covered artwork into a cardboard box that is around the same size as the artwork that has been wrapped in cardboard.

b. Add more cushioning material to the box to ensure that the artwork fits tightly Oversized cardboard layers and the artwork fitting snugly inside the box are what shield it from harm.

How Do Files Get Ready for Printing in Large Formats?

a. Adjust Pictures according to Viewing Distance.
b. Adjust the Screens.
c. Employ the Soft-Proofing feature in Photoshop.
d. Create Vectors from Fonts.
e. Save the File with the Correct Type

What dimensions do art prints have?

The following are some of the most popular sizes: 5x7, 8x10, 11x14, 16x20, 18x24, and 24x36 inches. The majority of art supply stores provide an even wider range of sizes.

EXPORTING FOR WEB AND SCREEN

When you export for the web, you can utilize sophisticated compression techniques to produce files that load much more quickly online by removing the color profile and any other metadata.

Unlike the conventional Save for Web dialog box, which only allowed users to export one artboard at a time and required them to repeat the process for each artboard they desired, the Export for Screens dialog box lets you export multiple artboards at once.

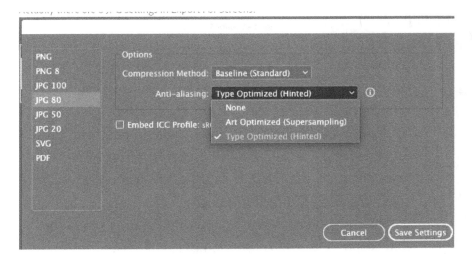

Export for screen

USING ADOBE BRIDGE FOR ASSET MANAGEMENT

A component of the Adobe Creative Cloud is Adobe Bridge. It facilitates the organization of the resources you utilize to produce print, digital, and video content. Adobe Bridge maintains readily accessible native Adobe files (such PSD and PDF) as well as non-Adobe assets.

A few typical operations, including producing contact sheets or web galleries, can be automated with Adobe Bridge,

COLLABORATING WITH OTHER ADOBE CREATIVE CLOUD APPS

along with making image previews and adding metadata to files. Using Adobe Creative Cloud's shared libraries to gain centralized access to content and maintain consistency across projects is essential to working together effortlessly. Making use of Adobe XD's collaborative tools promotes instantaneous feedback and iteration for more efficient design processes.

Efficient methods to use Adobe Creative Cloud for team collaboration?

1. As long as you have a working subscription and an internet connection, sync your files and settings. As a result, you may work on your projects from any location without having to worry about losing your preferences or data. You must use the Creative Cloud desktop application or the web interface and log into your Adobe account in order to sync your files and preferences.

2. Distribute your work and comments. Sharing your work and comments with team members is another option to use Adobe CC for collaboration. Depending on the kind of project and desired amount of interaction, there are various ways to go about doing this.

3. Employ Adobe Balance and Spark Stunning images, films, and web pages may be created and shared with the Adobe Spark online platform. It may be used to create flyers, posters, presentations, social media postings, and more.

4. Learn about Adobe Sensei and Premiere Rush, two machine learning tools that underpin some of Adobe CC's features and effects. It may be used to create new ideas, enhance quality, and automate operations.

5. Recognize and receive assistance You can utilize the tools and resources included with Adobe CC to learn and receive support.

TROUBLESHOOTING COMMON EXPORT ISSUES

In order to fix malfunctioning machines or systems, troubleshooting is a type of issue solving that is frequently used. Finding the root of an issue and fixing it to get the product or process back up and running again is a logical, methodical search.

Exporting can lead to errors. These are a few typical mistakes and actions:

1. All of the versions in Clear Case® VOBs are accessible using exporter commands. Make sure that there is enough disk space for the clear text pool on the VOB server.

2. Depending on how much data there is, the exporter command may take a while. Files and folders utilized by the exporter command in the dynamic view should not be accessed, checked out, or checked in. For routine tasks, you can utilize other Clear Case views.

3. Engineering Workflow Management (Engineering Workflow Management) is not accessible using the exporter command. During the export command, Engineering Workflow Management is capable of functioning.

4. After resolving the primary cause, you can try running the export command again.

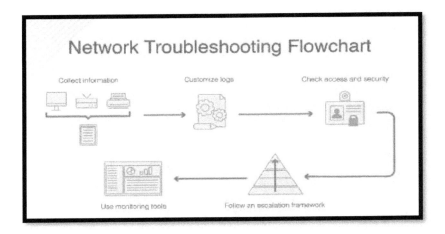

Chat of network troubleshooting.

INDEX

www.ingramcontent.com/pod-product-compliance
Lightning Source LLC
LaVergne TN
LVHW062035060326
832903LV00062B/1737